WORD STAFFORD

The First Retort

Various Authors

Edited by Mel Wardle Woodend

Cover Art and Poster Artwork by A Blind Photographer

WORD STAFFORD – THE FIRST RETORT

First Printing: 2022

ISBN: 978-1-7399337-7-7 (DREAM WELL WRITING LTD)

DREAM WELL WRITING LTD

STAFFORDSHIRE

UNITED KINGDOM

www.dreamwellwriting.simplesite.com

DREAM WELL

A Dyslexia Friendly Publication

DEDICATION

To every poet who took that first step up to the mic.

CONTENTS

Acknowledgements	Page 10
Introduction	Page 11
What Is WORD Stafford? And Who Are We?	Page 12
Testimonials	Page 15
SEASON ONE	Page 16
Episode One	Page 17
Episode Two	Page 18
Episode Three	Page 19
Episode Four	Page 19
Whose Apple Thou Art? – Deborah Edgeley	Page 20
Clown Face – Mark Sheeky	Page 21
Episode Five	Page 22
The Second Question – Mike Took	Page 22
Episode Six	Page 23
Episode Seven	Page 23
Moving On (from 1974) – Brendan Hawthorne	Page 24
Episode Eight	Page 26
The Farmer – Jason N Smith	Page 26
Episode Nine	Page 27
Naked – Chris Wilson	Page 27
Episode Ten – Season One Grand Final	Page 29

A Spider – Andy Wootton Page 29

Blind Johnny Smoke and Mel Wardle Woodend at Season One Episode Ten Grand Final Page 31

SEASON TWO Page 32

Episode One Page 33

Difficulty With Words – Sam Rapp Page 34

Episode Two Page 36

I Ran Away – Jordan Biddulph Page 37

Episode Three Page 38

Out of Luck Alice – Emilie Lauren Jones Page 39

Episode Four Page 42

Wembley at the Oval – Adrian McKenzie Page 43

Bubbles in the Sand – Al Barz Page 44

Episode Five Page 46

Arrest – Hannah Brockley Page 47

Episode Six Page 49

How Long Has Your Black Life Mattered – iLikeZach Page 50

The Daniel Kelleher Poem – Dwane Reads Page 54

World Poetry Day Page 55

Zoom Page 56

Episode Seven Page 57

What Makes This Sea Pool In? – Gerald Kells Page 58

Episode Eight Page 59

Episode Nine Page 59

Episode Ten – Season Two Grand Final Page 60

SEASON THREE Page 61

Episode One Page 62

I Am Not a Robot – Ann Atkins Page 63

The Cannabis Anarchist – Willis the Poet Page 65

Episode Two Page 67

And Counting.... – Cathi Rae Page 67

Episode Three Page 69

The Summer Chill – Wesley Rolston Page 69

Episode Four Page 70

Episode Five Page 70

Big Sister – Lisa Millard Page 71

The Port 'N' Cigar Club Fund – Paul Eccentric Page 72

Episode Six Page 74

If Hope is the Thing with Feathers – Claire Hughes Page 75

Episode Seven Page 78

Choices – Lisa Johnston Page 79

Episode Eight Page 81

Edge to Edge – Ashley Edge Page 82

Final Journey – Angie Payne Page 85

Fisherman's Moon – Joanna Smart Page 87

That day – Emma Purshouse	Page 89
Episode Nine	Page 91
A Terraced House, Bolebridge Tamworth 1884 – Jan Hedger	Page 92
Happy Child – Janet Jenkins	Page 93
On the Beach – Sarah Dale	Page 94
Embryo – Susan Wood	Page 95
Episode Ten – Season Three Grand Final	Page 96
Blind Johnny Smoke and Mel Wardle Woodend at Season Three Episode Ten Grand Final on Zoom	Page 96
How Can We Trust the System – Daniel Kay	Page 97
Ciudad de Sevilla – Pauline Faulkner	Page 99
Defences – Kizzy Wade	Page 100
JUDGES' POEMS	Page 102
Seashell – Sandra Mary Chambers	Page 103
Loss – Lily Massey	Page 104
Flowers – Uschi Wheeler	Page 105
Ocean Whispers – Katy Watkiss	Page 106
SOMETHING FROM THE HOSTS	Page 109
Grenfell 2017-2019 – Mel Wardle Woodend	Page 110
Tin – Blind Johnny Smoke	Page 113
OTHER THINGS	Page 115
Stafford Walking Street with Guide Dog / Poetry Dog JJ	Page 116

Positive Poetry and Poems Page 117

World Book Night Page 117

Staffordshire Day Page 117

Myths and Legends Page 118

Mental Health Awareness Week Page 119

World Oceans Day Page 119

Empathy Day Page 119

World Poetry Day Book Launch Page 120

The Festival of Hope Page 121

Black Lives Matter Page 121

Alzheimer's Awareness Poetry Night Page 121

Dyslexia Awareness Poetry Night Page 122

National Poetry Day Page 122

Competitions Page 123

Christmas Party Page 123

Bonus Material – Echoes Poetry Film Page 125

Biographies Page 126

About WORD Stafford Page 127

Dream Well Writing Ltd Page 128

ACKNOWLEDGEMENTS

Thank you to all our supporters who help to make WORD Stafford what it is – with particular thanks to our judges and special guests, Stafford Library, Stafford District Arts Council, The Bird in Hand Stafford, our lovely performers and audience, and Mel's Mum Tricia for her unwavering support and delicious cakes.

We are grateful to all the poets who have sent us their work to publish in this anthology. Without their generosity, the book would not have been possible!

Please note, poems included are not necessarily those performed on the night.

INTRODUCTION

A compendium of poetry from slam winners, special guests and supporters from the first three seasons of WORD Stafford: a regular spoken word event held in the county town, that transferred onto Zoom during the Covid-19 pandemic lockdowns and is now held as a hybrid in person event that is also streamed on Zoom.

WORD Stafford provides a safe space for new and experienced poets alike to enjoy sharing their work in front of a warm and supportive audience and the purpose of the anthology is partly to tell our story and raise awareness of the importance of spoken word and community events, to advertise and promote the fabulous poets within its pages – creating a permanent home for the poems within, and indeed a sense of permanence for our event. We will additionally be able to raise much needed funds for our event through any sales made - so that we may purchase promotional equipment when necessary and to fund guest payments and event prizes.

The First Retort is edited by Mel Wardle Woodend Staffordshire Poet Laureate 2019-2022 with cover artwork by A Blind Photographer - the hosts and organisers of WORD Stafford.

WHAT IS WORD STAFFORD?

AND

WHO ARE WE?

WORD Stafford began life as a poetry slam named 'Word Shrapnel' and was first thought up and implemented by local poet, Adam Probert. After a few months of running a successful slam in the function room of The Bird in Hand pub in Stafford, Adam moved onto other things and rather than see the end of Stafford's only regular poetry event Blind Johnny Smoke and I took the reins and began to revamp the event to be the WORD Stafford you see and know today at Stafford Library, on Zoom and at a number of other welcoming local venues.

I sometimes cannot quite believe that I am at my most confident standing in front of a microphone, hosting a poetry event and finding things to say on the spot with ease – when only a couple of years earlier I would not have had the confidence to even walk into a pub alone to meet friends, or to speak up in a work meeting, let alone ever dream I would enjoy standing up in front of a room full of people hosting an event! I used to be absolutely terrified of speaking up in front of people! But I ABSOLUTELY LOVE IT and have found that behind a mic is one of the places where I feel most comfortable, confident and at home.

I think it helps that near to the beginning of my spoken word journey in 2017 and on finding friendships, support and encouragement from poets like Adam and Jon I learnt to finally accept myself the way I am as 'ME' without feeling the need to hide my mental health troubles or pretend to be something I am not. 'The truth is' as a line in one of my poems says, 'I have OCD – and now I am not afraid of being me, I am free…' (*Just a Thought*, 2019) and that certainly reflects in the confidence I have found in the poetry scene.

Jon is a great friend and such fun to run a poetry event with. I am the bossy one, whereas he is the calm, collected one who makes me see reason and another point of view if I am cross or impatient about anything at WORD. He is also the technical one who does all the magical things with the equipment that I don't understand, and all the artwork for posters and for our book! He is an incredibly kind and creative person – and I know that when one of us has an idea, we don't just talk about it as a pipe dream, but both have the motivation to work hard to put it into action and create lots of opportunities for other people to enjoy, as well as having fun ourselves. I think the main thing that I enjoy about WORD is that we just have fun! There are no airs and graces. We are just ourselves – standing in front of a room full of friends, acquaintances, and often strangers – and hoping to make them feel welcome and included. We don't take ourselves too seriously and hopefully create a relaxed, yet professional event where people can have fun but hopefully also find that WORD Stafford is a place they can come to be valued as individuals, have their words listened to, be encouraged to write and create, learn and grow.

Mel Wardle Woodend
Staffordshire Poet Laureate 2019-2022 and
Director of Dream Well Writing Ltd

I was lucky enough to be along for the ride when Word Shrapnel and another varied open mic night called The Powder Keg were active in Stafford. Both events were masterminded by punk poet Adam Probert, a legendary human that I am privileged to call one of my closest friends. Our journey continues with spoken word/power noise act The Mannequin Factory, but I digress.

I was struck that in Word Shrapnel I was seeing and partaking in something unique and a type of culture that I don't think Stafford had ever experienced. When this event concluded I saw a very real possibility that this blaze of culture would simply extinguish. After chatting to Mel, I think we had both reached the same conclusion that we couldn't let this happen. With Adam's blessing we tweaked a few things and WORD was born.

I saw myself as a facilitator really, rather than seeking it as a platform for my own art. A safe and welcoming platform for anyone wanting to explore performance poetry and spoken word. I am and always will be a musician and sound artist at heart, though WORD has allowed me to develop my writing and delivery in new ways. Importantly for me, as someone who is severely deaf and going increasingly blind over time, spoken word performance has been more achievable and less stressful than playing with bands in dark and noisy venues, and for this I am very grateful. I still don't think I deserve to be called a poet, I'm just a punk shouty person.

The greatest reward though is seeing a huge variety of individuals (both local and international, thanks to the magic of Zoom) find and embrace WORD as part of their lives. Mel and I have seen people getting solace and support by being part of the WORD family, establishing new friendships and developing as artists. Mel too has become a close friend who is always there through thick and thin. These things give me a warm feeling inside and so I am proud and privileged to be a part of the WORD team.

Blind Johnny Smoke

TESTIMONIALS

'Word Stafford has been a very inclusive and welcoming environment for me and many others and has given me many opportunities to help charities in any way I can through anthology projects and fund-raisers. Very much a spoken word group that cares for both its participants and whomever they are raising funds for… …a wonderful family of poetry and spoken word enthusiasts.' **– Jordan Biddulph, Poet.**

'WORD Stafford are amazing - they kept us all connected and creative during COVID lockdown and boosted our mental health. They are wonderful human beings who give generously to the poetry community, support local charities and provide a platform for wordsmiths. Two sentences is not enough to describe my admiration - and debt - to Mel and Jon. Big respect and thank you for all that you do.' **– Ian Henery, Walsall Poet Laureate.**

'WORD Stafford will blow ya socks off and soothe your head in the same evening.' **– Andy Wootton, Performance Poet.**

SEASON

ONE

EPISODE ONE

Someone (probably Mel) did not think to begin keeping records of WORD Stafford until AFTER Episode One, which began one Saturday evening in early summer, 2018 at The Bird in Hand pub in Stafford town centre. The first 'home' of WORD.

We know lots of people attended and had a good time – and we know there was a winner – Phillip Knight (1st place) – and then when Episode Two came along, we realized it might be a sensible idea to document everything on Facebook so the WORD Facebook page was created by Blind Johnny Smoke and all subsequent posters, photographs and write ups of the events have appeared there.

Please do check it out at **@WORDstafford**

EPISODE TWO

Joint 1st Place - Derek Baker and Pattie Tunnicliffe

EPISODE THREE

1st Place – Nick Degg

EPISODE FOUR

1st Place – Andy Wootton

Whose Apple Thou Art?

In Greenwood, studded with crab and perry,
out of tempest mind tumbled Caliban.
So say yeomen of sixteenth century,
'Bring thee where the crabs grow,' said the madman.
Drinking proverbial acidity,
Gossip's Bowl was spice sipped by Bidford folk,
in restaurants of ancient forestry
acid draughts intoxicate shallow jokes.
But three crabbed months had soured themselves to death.
'He'll never have Miranda,' they concurred.
The Bidford souls muttered under their breath
'Goddess and a madman?' with spoon they stirred.
'Whose apple thou art, gem grown from deep root?'
'Yours, but I will never bear sweet fruit.'

Deborah Edgeley – Special Guest: Fall In Green

Clown Face

Crushed into beetles' petals, for my lips
I can feel their sun, encased in the austere lacquer
and made into a paste for laughter.

Something like my father's face, romanced
with a rim of lightbulbs, and tears of his hope
walks a well-worn script.

Where Aztecs ruled, a child-hand curtseys,
and a tent of insects applaud the basket,
their bloody farewell crying a smile
to the Northern rain in my heart.

The glitter thrown to the wind falls to the dust of saws.
Stars to ashes, heaven's applause.

Mark Sheeky – Special Guest: Fall In Green

EPISODE FIVE

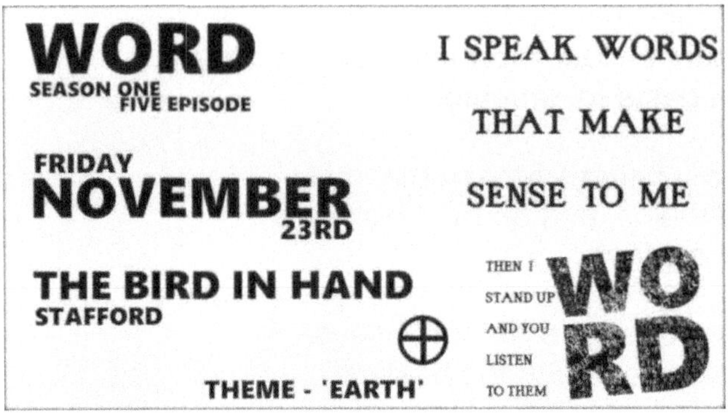

OPEN MIC

The Second Question

This is a poem celebrating diversity in our culture, but lamenting how sometimes the need to demonstrate that diversity simply manifests itself as a box-ticking accountability exercise. It is not a slam poem, but was written for and featured in my 2018 Edinburgh Fringe show "Overpriced Zeitgeist".

I'm a non-British resident, transgender working pensioner
I'm a means-tested, mixed race, unpaid contracted support-worker
I'm a non-white, gender fluid, single parent lesbian
I'm a child of Muslim parents, asexual, agnostic, churchgoer

Review my application
Process my claim
Specify my future
But struggle with my name
Confirm my entitlement
Deal with my request
Govern my choices
Decide what happens next

I'm an angry retired socialist considering private medicine
I'm a genius adolescent who's been taught to hate society
I'm a childless unemployed father with some kids who call me Dad
I'm a dyslexic mature student filling forms in for a loan

Rejected? Deferred?
Your final word
Approved? Denied?
You decide
Adopted? Non-practising? Queer? Two mothers?
Just put "Other"
Tick the box
Be judged by a social paradox

Oh how I want to fit in
To be happy and successful just doing my thing
You ask, I answer
But what can I do
If the second question always means I have to justify myself
To you?

Mike Took

EPISODE SIX

1ST Place – Jane James

EPISODE SEVEN

1ST Place – Daron Carey

Moving On (from 1974)

This is a poem about identity and identifying with a particular place. My first thirteen years of life were spent living in South Staffs. My area of the Black Country (the bit south of the South Staffordshire coal fields) was called that then. I actually lived in a shire! Unfortunately, in 1974 I was one of many who were Metropolitanised, moved without changing address.

When I was young, my dad regularly took me to the Potteries on school holidays as he worked around the six towns. The smell of industry and the dusting of clay gave the area a fusty, dusty smell and a ghostly appearance. Memories of the hunched bottle kilns, shadowy in twilight have stayed with me to this day.

Interestingly, The Metropolitan Borough of Sandwell also consists of six towns!

They moved the borders
when I was asleep
Changed my address
without a removal van
Moved me from a shire
to a borough
Qualified
Quantified
Metropolitanised me
with a stroke of a pen
and a push of a button
Made an amalgam of me
Homogenised the six home towns
into collective individuality
Sacrificed their history
like pawns in a chess game
that left us all
in a stalemate state of
fug-bound decay
We became
a broken window on a page
A jagged hole
left by lines on a map
that didn't meet up

A place where the cracks were taped up
and decorated with bejewelled ring roads
only to become choked up expressways
merely allowing 1st gear
A landlocked post-industrial desert
with confusing signage
around well-known potholes
and ever-increasing roadworks
And if you ever need Sandwell and Dudley train station
just try looking in Oldbury
My drinking water
comes from South Staffs taps
when it's really from Wales
My Black Country phone number
is exchanged in Birmingham
My postcode is
stamped in Walsall
My electricity for now
is from France
and I don't know who I am
or where I'm from anymore
Sandwell isn't on a map
It's a concept
A name
A logo rebrand
and a place where the people
are proud of their past
but the Staffordshire knot
still remains oddly
upside down

Brendan Hawthorne – Special Guest
Wednesbury Poet Laureate

EPISODE EIGHT

The Farmer

The farmer sees hidden slithering's
flipping slick coils in the dark,
beyond hedged boundaries
long laid down to demark.

He sees icy hail descending from skies,
thunder, lightning and rain flooding fields,
but the seeds, whom he must shield,
they do not see.

Seeds,

seated within the warm embrace of earth,
nurtured and secured in strength
and hope contained in the composition of a life
Eternally laid down before them.

They thrust forth shoots,
they reach though cracks to grab
rays of light,

they reach high to glory in day
and suckle on morning dew,

longing to grow exude vibrant hue,

and bloom, but

I wonder, do you see the farmer
tending to you?

1st Place – Jason N Smith

EPISODE NINE

Naked

You said that you were scared
That you'd be embarrassed

You need not have worried

I remember, hearing the air leave the room as the door opened
As you used your key for the first time, lock and heart opened
I remember the look in your eyes
Trepidation and expectance
Desire tempered by reality

You glide like smoke across the floor. Tangible, visible and lingering
Filling lungs, saturating heart and blood, coursing through to extremities
As hands reach out, to pull filter tip to lip, laced with poison and exhilaration
Each moment, resting on the purse, danger and unknown pleasures. This division of joy and terrors

Stimulated, vascular pulses cause coursing swollen vessels
Pupils widen, eager to learn, to know more, to seek out truths
Hidden

Breath deepens, the gaps between them span the incremental distance of each step that brings us closer

And Closer

Closer

'til polar attraction, magnetic assurance brings nicotine teased lips together

As hungry hands diet on the small of your back.
Too aware to feast. Too hungry to abstain
Eyes drink in each exposed inch
Flesh
Goosebumps, not of cold design but of cold resignation
That this is now and this is happening

To hold back, to fight this realisation, this culmination of kindred spirits
The futility as this spark, as kindling catches hold of flame, warms two bodies,
Coiled, tightly wound like frenzied springs in wait for kinetic release

You were not alone

You need not have worried

I see you, I see you for what you are

And You, you are beautiful

1st Place – Chris Wilson

EPISODE TEN – SEASON ONE GRAND FINAL

A Spider

There's a spider in the bath!

"Is it definitely a spider and not the green bit off the top of a tomato...like you used to throw in for a lark, when we were first married?"

(That bit's true)

No it's a spider, a big one!
It was indeed a spider, a very big one.
I put down a wet razor for scale and went to fetch my camera.
When I came back, she had lit candles and shaved her legs.
All of them.
"Thanks" she duskily exhaled.
There'll be no bath night for me tonight, I thought.
And I bet she'll block the plughole with spidery-stubble.
Then with a twinkle in her eyes, eyes, eyes,
She drew me closer with a sultry beckon.
"Come and loof my back with a loofah" she said.
Any particular luc luc luc luxury bath creme?
"Something sweet to bring in the prey"

So I loofed her back with essence of honeydew, or, something,
Before she brazenly step, step, step, stepped out.
"Towel?" she smouldered.
Theeee green one, I shakily pointed.
Then she began to spin me around and bind me up tight.
"You'll keep" she said, "'til later tonight"
And via the bathroom window, she went out, on the lash.
Hearing now my muffled plea,
My wife came up to cut me free,
She couldn't help but to agree
That this,
Was no tomato top.
We had no choice, we had to douse and petrol bomb the entire house.
Insured, we then decide to roam and bought a little mobile home
And if horizons looked eight-leggéd,
The other way's where we were headed.
In hope that she would never knock, the entrance to the shower block.
When I'm wearing my wife's pink bathrobe,
A newly diagnosed arachnophobe.

1st Place – Andy Wootton
Season One Grand Champion

Blind Johnny Smoke and Mel Wardle Woodend
at
Season One Episode Ten Grand Final

SEASON

TWO

EPISODE ONE

1st Place – Carys Hannah

Difficulty With Words

I have Difficulty with words, so they said!

I pronounce them wrong, sometimes,
I hear birds singing but not in order, I love nature's disorder.

I have difficulty with maths, they said!
As I cannot see the numbers, but I do see them in a different way.

I think it's society, trying to make things awkward so it's not actually me, because when someone says, "What's wrong with you"? I say nothing, I'm just being me! So, as I was saying,

Maths and numbers, do make perfect sense, just not in any dictated structure, so when you ask me about the alphabet, and what's 30 metres and say in your sarcastic tone you surely know your times tables? I don't mean to moan but...
No! I don't!

I'm very happy with that, because I am visual and see things differently in harmony with nature's lands, as they jump out to me in patterns of formations, like starlings above Brighton Pier, dancing in the skies, around me, putting on an acrobatic display that only, I can see, I think that's magical wizardry, just for me.

I have word blindness, but I can see,

I struggle to spell, but can spell, Sometimes round the wrong way, but I know their meaning as the words are my very soul and being, I have no difficulty in what they want to say, they are arranged around in a different way, there is nothing wrong with that.

I have difficulty with words, so I am told, but I don't think so,
I have difficulty with words but still pass exams,

I have difficulty with words, but who told me that?

Grammar is this way and spelt like that, but who said that?
Shakespeare, in his first folios didn't use grammar, and he wrote lots of plays, poems, sonnets, now that's pretty great, he made us,

laugh, cry, and quiver in your seat if it's Lady Macbeth, or Titus Andronicus with their bloody ways, to greet.

Spelling and grammar has different ways, for a story to unfold but not your conventional ways,

My letters re- arrange, like toy soldiers lined up, ready for play, and jump out at me, when they have something to say, screaming sometimes, is what they do, which is somewhat rude when they tell me, it's got to be written this way, not like that, and although we have our disagreements, I'm ok with that, in our little splat, but I don't care, if I'm am slower, than them, I am not in their dispeare, I am not in despair.

My letters that make words are ok, even if they are upside down, they are not muddled to me
I can spell, how many times do I have to yell, there is spell check and software that helps.

So, you say.

I have difficulty with words,

But I don't have any difficulty at all, because I have got rid of any curses from witches' spells, being Dyslexic, being Dyspraxic, being Dyscalculia is just swell and in my world it's all just me and that's Amazingly Dyslexic and great, can't you see.

Sam Rapp – Special Guest: The Dyslexic Poet

EPISODE TWO

WORD 2
WORD - SEASON TWO EPISODE TWO
FRIDAY 30TH AUGUST 2019
8PM
'FICTION!'
FREE ENTRY
POETRY SLAM! AND OPEN MIC
WITH SPECIAL GUEST, WRITER
NIGEL HUTCHINSON!
BIRD IN HAND STAFFORD

I Ran Away

I came from a town of broken promises.
Where each brick was cemented with pain,
mixed with tears and roughhousing.
It's not a one in a million tale.
It's a story shared with many.
Each hand will say something different,
in their lines of fate.
Yet they are all scarred the same.

I needed to discover who I was,
I travelled. Leaving those bricks behind.
All that pain, to search for who I am.
instead of bringing what I was with me.
Exploring the world in the search for my own utopia of self.

The realization came sudden.
During years of travel,
'There is no utopia for me, is there?'
Every place had its welcoming communities.
But not one allowed my broken jigsaw body to fit.

But it was fine, the pain subsided.
I got to know others along my travels,
they had come to the realization also.
They stopped traveling,
instead of looking, they started building.
Their tears and sweat cemented bricks of hope.

I travelled home, tired and optimistic.
I took one of the bricks in a broken wall.
Cracked it open, with great difficulty.
And there hidden inside,
was hope all along.

Jordan Biddulph – Joint 2nd Place

EPISODE THREE

1st Place – Emilie Lauren Jones

Out of Luck Alice

Caterpillar was on his second cigar.
Alice, down to her last fiver
watched hazy mist surround her,
cloud her from underpaid rent
and overpaid men.
Smoke swirled, turning into points
around stilettoes
that the adverts told her to wear.

Caterpillar motioned her over
with twelve of his arms,
offered her a pitcher
in exchange for a picture.

Well, thought Alice,
It's only a picture.

Maybe you think it's only a drink
but if you ignore your prejudice
against Alices who rely on juices
and half-smoked spliffs
to assist in the fight against
too small homes
with windows that don't close,

concrete gardens set on the margins
of a society run by blue ties
and the BBC who only every feature
where you live when there's a stabbing,
then maybe you'll start to understand
where Alice is going.

Caterpillar had a hundred hands,
asked if he could put three on her lap
in exchange for a full pack of fags
and ten pounds.

Well, thought Alice,
It's only a few hands,
out of a whole caterpillar of arms.

Maybe you think it's only fags and a tenner
but if you've never lived
with a fridge that's in the red
and a bed that's a mattress on the floor,
with your last blood-spotted note
rolled into the foetal position
in your purse then...

Caterpillar educated Alice
about five-bedroom yachts

and where's best to stay in Vegas
and how it's advisable to take lessons
before you take to ski slopes
and would she mind coming back to his
to lie naked on lettuce,
blow smoke rings
while he cocoons her
in exchange for shoes better than those,
a working credit card, weekend away...

Well, thought Alice,
It's only me.
Maybe you think –
but you don't, do you?
You don't like thinking about Alice.

Emilie Lauren Jones – 1st Place
Coventry Poet Laureate 2021 – 2023

EPISODE FOUR

1st Place – Adrian McKenzie

Wembley at the Oval

Before rain stops play
Take the ball and spin it past your posts.
Past keepers of old scores and goals
Past makers of mounds and moulds
Bounce it so hard they duck and you break yours
Guardian angels, serendipitous saviours
Field favours like spring weddings
Take the ball and spread it in every direction
Passing jams like your sat nav
Greased palms don't always make for great catches
Run after what matters
Shedding blocks at every line of scrimmage
Your circle's centre doesn't have to have you in it.
See worlds and be water until the land is in view
Eat trigger stew if you've the appetite to handle it
Applaud other's pressured passages
Play percentages for averages even when yours is banterous
Know that when you're engaged, momentary marriages are manageable, momentous and magnanimous
Old Spice can't always create classics and our links might die in battle but if we're on the field then maybe ours is the day
So what will you do before the rain stops play

Adrian McKenzie – 1st Place

Bubbles in the Sand

gold-glistened sunshine beaches
desiccated by tropical breezes
ripples coagulated by slapping tides
ideal spot for an hour's amusement
children, excitement, pots and small spades
parents watching undimmed joys
smooth nugacious castles collapsed
young life enticed by sudden mysteries
owning freedom like bubbles in the sand

and there look, there is a Boy
not sharing, far from parents' calls
not dressed for a beach but He doesn't care
not expecting right now to be there
in His neat shirt, shorts, socks and small shoes
for His interrupted journey to His new beginning
the ocean has returned Him - pushed Him up the beach
soft tides whisper in the quiet afternoon
“anah la yantami huna” - "He does not belong here."
if only He could see, face down, sudden mysteries,
owning freedom like bubbles in the sand

more years of wasted broadcasts
display still the hate-cloud skies
above those who are 'not us'
scream “go home” from a going-nowhere bus
a pulpit that markets methods to madmen
methods speaking lies above other skies
mad hate to rain on peaceful heads
on lifetimes eked in lands we dare not smell
such courage to abandon hope
to brave an empty fleedom with a beautiful child
our freedom's entrails scattered on societies
our freedom like bubbles in their sand

on this beach no tracks ebb or flow
no hand brought this broken beauty,
settled as sediment on the rim of a cup
vain hope's evanescing watermark
a divorced consequence of remote control
decisions in far and obdurate minds
busting freedom like bubbles in the sand
where once lay a boy

Al Barz – Joint 2nd Place

EPISODE FIVE

1st Place – Hannah Brockley

Arrest

A beep in my ear
then noises unclear:
"Ambulance service is the patient breathing?"
"Oh god, I don't know!" you scream as you're heaving.
I take your address
trying not to show stress
as you rush your location
in panic and frustration
and have to confirm it
while coming to terms with it.
"She fell from the top stair
and now she's just lying there
this is more than I can bear
oh god, oh god, this just isn't fair!"
"I know how much you must care,
that this is your worst nightmare,
but there's no time to waste,
check for signs of life without haste."
It doesn't seem real
as you look, listen, feel.
You fear for her death
when you can't feel her breath
"Start CPR without delay,
I've already got crews on the way,
I'm going to tell you what to do,
don't worry I'll stay on the line with you."
You start the compressions
with a little aggression
but they need to be hard
to make her heart start.
Pushing on her chest hard and fast,
wondering if her last breath was really her last.
Counting out with you every PUSH, PUSH, PUSH,
mapping the cars making scene in a rush.
"She's breathing!" you yell, voice cracked with shock.
Compressions being echoed by the tick-ticking of the clock.
"OK, just check – are her breaths even?"

Maybe this girl will give us something to believe in.
“She’s breathing normally” – you sigh, with relief?
Strange how your voice is still panged with grief.
“Roll her onto her side, no pillow or cushion-“
my advice cut short by the sound of you hushing.
“Stop talking my love, you just need to rest.”
A quiver in your voice, stained with distress.
“No pillows or cushions under her head.”
Then, at that moment, I heard what she said.
She grabbed at the chance to set herself free
when she murmured - just loud enough – “You – pushed – me”.

Hannah Brockley – 1st Place

EPISODE SIX

1st Place – iLikeZach

How Long Has Your Black Life Mattered

We've been saying Black lives matter
Since before it was a hashtag

We've been saying Black lives matter since it sounded like something else
Other words, other worlds away

Dragging chains that kept us sardine packed in the bottom of English ships for months on end
And with a taste of daylight mid-trip
Wrapping those chains
Around our waists and our necks
And falling gracefully off those decks into the sea
With the precious names of our African gods on our lips
Whispering to those deities just before the waves hit us
'You will remember us
I know you will
Even if Jesus won't'
That's how Black lives matter used to sound

See we've been saying Black lives matter
Since before it was a hashtag

Ever since it sounded like a so-called slave
Estranged in a strange land

A grown man

Beaten and tortured and terrorised

The word they used at the time was 'broken'

And given the token name of some Ancient Greek or Shakespearean character

Thus characterising this individual as a figment

A shadow to be pleasing or offensive, rather than a human being

The Negro Orpheus. Castor, a slave with strong legs. Benvolio, a buck, also from the Ivory Coast.

Sold this day from Atlanta in the colonies to St. Barthélemy in the West Indies

To correct troublesome behaviour.

Black lives matter used to sound like "troublesome behaviour"

We've been saying Black lives matter

Since before it was a hashtag

Before gas bags from Fox News and the BBC sat on their evening high horses

And debated the merits and respectable limits and the reasonable tones that should exemplify

A revolution of thought

Imagine the colossal waste

In putting on a suit

Sitting at a news desk

Shuffling papers

And placing an accusatory index finger to one's ear just to say

This just in

We don't love you

And we don't think your life was worth a damn anyway

More on this after these commercial messages

I know you stayed up all night stencilling out the image on a protest poster

With a closed sable hand perfectly centered

With the thumb going symmetrically over the knuckles

The perfect picture of solidarity and allyship

But we've been saying Black lives matter ever since the image was 3D printed in real-time

As an actual raised Black fist

Black lives matter used to sound like the soft illegal hiss

Of 'Rest in Power Forever' written in spray paint on a wall

Next to the best image of a fallen brother or sister that the ghetto could muster

Along with his or her birth and death year

And every so often a disillusioned grandmother would sit in front of that mural in a plastic deck chair

And hang her head sideways balanced on her fist

And look up to the sky wondering how it ever came to this

Black lives matter used to sound like

Her thoughts wandering

Trying to calculate the psychological cost

Over the course of her 60 years

From having to constantly hear again and again the news of

Another Black life lost, another Black life lost, another Black life lost

Black lives matter used to sound like her silence in that chair

Knowing so much

Having so much she could say

But wondering what in the hell for?

We've been saying Black lives matter

Since before it was a hashtag

And I'm so thankful that it doesn't sound like silence anymore

iLikeZach – 1st Place

The Daniel Kelleher Poem

Another overhead shell winds past death fields
Sending once confident men towards madness
Shattered, but not broken, they await their call
oh, Mercy upon child soldiers allowed to enlist

on the sound of a sergeant's whistle, be ready
As Bayonets fixed our eyes close in silence
wooden ladders with not the fear of heights
flesh hanging on the wire, a feast for crows

minutes become hours until hours didn't matter
men wounded lay muted moments before death
praise our stretcher bearers' nightly manoeuvres
pulling from the slurry of a shell blast waste land

welcome, city of canvas tents that never sleeps
men irrespective of background being assessed
all operating tables manned by foreign surgeons
hidden behind enemy lines without prejudice.

brush in hand sent for rehabilitation to Hamburg
a daily contribution towards the war effort here
words became sentences turning to conversation
those missing in action lives sadly never fulfilled

Dwane Reads – 2nd Place

WORLD POETRY DAY

We were all looking forward to celebrating World Poetry Day with a writing group called The Stone Scribblers – at Stone Library – with poems written in different forms from a number of countries and cultures around the world…

…but in March 2020 the COVID-19 Pandemic arrived in the UK and we all went into Lockdown.

We put our thinking caps on…

and WORD Stafford's World Poetry Day Celebration

went from this

to this!

ZOOM

We wanted to keep the poetry community of Staffordshire as connected as possible – and ironically – whilst everyone was PHYSICALLY isolated, locked down and shielding in their own homes and gardens, the poetry community felt closer than ever because Zoom allowed people to connect who had previously had distance, or disability, or travel issues, or other reasons that created a barrier to attending events in person.

Although COVID-19 itself has been a terrible experience for so many, learning about and adapting to putting events online on Zoom opened up the poetry community of Staffordshire and welcomed in the world.

EPISODE SEVEN

1st Place – Gerald Kells

What Makes This Sea Pool In?

First published in LI Poems

what makes this sea pool in
and in the still bay rumble over
itself, as rhythmic as the softening
beat of those who pass, hidden
by rock-crests and under trees
on stunted upper cliffs from which
silence out-plays and small birds
whistle and larger birds climb?

what holds this pooling in of turquoise
between deep maroon or, further out,
beyond the bit-ends of rock,
a stretching back to where the
waves start from a single, glimpsed line,
sketch-made, rubbed-clean,
uncharcoaled, always?

Gerald Kells – 1st Place

EPISODE EIGHT

1st Place – Andy Summers

EPISODE NINE

1st Place – Priyanka Joshi

EPISODE TEN – SEASON TWO GRAND FINAL

Season Two Grand Champion – Priyanka Joshi

SEASON

THREE

EPISODE ONE

1st Place – Andy Summers

I Am Not a Robot

I know I'm not. I can tick a box to prove I’m not.
I think I'm not… should I have ticked that box?
My body is more complex than any man-made machine:
just a few parts are malfunctioning.
My brain is more powerful than any computer,
although I could use an upgrade to my processor.
My decision making is slowww and lacking clarity.

Perhaps I need to do a clean-up, run a utility,
defrag my hard drive.
There are a few files I'd like to wipe,
but I’ll have to quarantine
‘cos I don’t want to delete something I might need;
others I wish I could recall with ease
instead of randomly accessing unpleasant memories.

I’d like to reset my display, brighten the colours,
remove a few lines and dots,
see if I can change the settings to 'smile more often'.
I think my default face got corrupted and forgot.
I'm definitely in need of a software upgrade,
not sure what version number I'm on,
this one is prone to bugs, bugs, bugs and crashes,
put under pressure, often freezes;
is hard to get off standby, especially in the morning,
shuts down without warning,

Sleep Mode not set to the correct timezone:
awake in the early hours, sometimes I wish I was a robot
and I could just switch off.

Perhaps it's that my expectations are wrong.
I'm trying to fit a niche where I don't belong.
Working too long at full capacity
destroyed a few cells.
The stress on my body is definitely starting to tell.

Maybe I'm not meant for a corporate expansion slot
because I am not a robot:
not a sum of my faults, a failure log,
marked beyond economic repair, obsolete.
It's my flaws that make me unique.

So why should I think I need to be good at everything?
After all, nobody expects to cook a meal
in a washing machine.

I can hold your hand when you're sad or worried,
make you a sandwich the way you like it if you're hungry,
bring you a perfectly brewed cup of tea.
I want to celebrate my creativity.
I don't want to stay in safe mode.
I don't need a factory reset.

I'm me.

Ann Atkins – Joint 2nd Place

The Cannabis Anarchist

A poem inspired by the story of a 74-Year-Old man arrested for giving his church congregation cookies laced with cannabis

He pops up at social occasions
Where there is a heartfelt need
For community based donations
And a lot of hungry mouths to feed

He brings his secret stash
Inside its Tupperware
His cookies baked with hash
For everyone to share

He's bought some lemon sherbet dabs
And stuck to all the dipping lollies
Hallucinogenic acid tabs
In about an hour they'll be off their trollies

Inside his chocolate éclair
His modified crème fraiche
Delivers a thousand yard stare
Brought on by crystal meth

He's put Uppers in the cuppas
Kibbles in the nibbles
Rohypnol in the Arctic Roll
And Wack in all the flap jack
There's Purple Haze in the canapes

Peruvian Flake in the carrot cake
He's even laced the margarine
With A grade street sourced Benzadrine
And to feed his need
For the sharing of joy
He's put Crazy Weed
In the saveloy

There's rock in all the rock cakes
Cake in all the other cakes
Temazepam in the breaded ham
Ketamine in the strawberry jam
He's spiked the tea with LSD
The sandwiches with Ecstasy
There's even Acapulco Red
In his freshly baked banana bread

He's a one man pharmacologist
The UK's Walter White
An all star Congregationalist
Doing what he thinks is right

So to help us all I've pulled some strings
And though it seems preposterous
He's down to do the catering
At the Tory Party Conference

Willis the Poet – Special Guest

EPISODE TWO

1st Place – Hannah Brockley

And Counting....

And at 12 my daughter starts to spread her wings
Her chosen companions on shopping trips
Her mates.... Not me
So
There are rules.... stay together.... don't talk to boys
If all else fails and you're frightened or things fall apart
Go find someone in a uniform they're there to help you

White privilege

In a clapped-out car seen many better days
And a brake light that flickers on and off and on
I get pulled over.... So.... I smile
Ratch up my accent a notch or two
Invent a wholly fictitious husband who fails to fix the simplest thing
Waved on and told to get it sorted soon

White privilege

Our house burgled
Every room ransacked
Every drawer undone
The police arrive.... Solicitous
Armed with window stickers
And contact details for a charity that gives support
The officer strategically choses to ignore the stench of weed
That sneaks from under my adult daughter's door

White privilege

Watching my best friend's son preparing for a big night out
Suit sharp.... Trainers just so
And we worry
Well of course we worry
Worry that he might get drunk
Worry that he might get laid
Worry that he might get involved in some scuffle in a night club car park

White privilege

And years ago
Burdened with babies and bags
And a buggy whose back wheel sticks
I fail to see that my child has helped herself to a small plush bear
Until half way home
So…. Of course we turn
A lesson to be learnt
Ignore the chorus of wails and tears
And in the shop
They're charmed
Insist she keeps the toy

White privilege

So intent on conversation with a man I hoped might be a lover
We left the coffee shop didn't pay our bill
But
No pavement pounding pursuit for us

White privilege

Lost on a leafy lane
We stopped to ask the gardening guy for help
And he unsure
Summoned his wife from deep indoors
For further knowledge reinforcement
Then asked how our holiday was going
Recommended a nearby pub that welcomes dogs

White privilege

Never asked where I come from
Never asked where I really really really come from
No badly disguised surprise at my use of words
Or my ability to solve a cryptic crossword clue

White privilege

And on
And on
And on.

Cathi Rae – Special Guest

EPISODE THREE

1st Place – Wesley Rolston

The Summer Chill

In this moment I feel unable.
I look intensely, obsessively at the chipped wooden table.
I think I see the sun setting outside.
Or I don't, I'm not sure, this creaking desk chair is where I reside.
I force my hand to rise to drink, but I can't, I'm weary.
Instead, I touch the cold metal of the object in front of me.
I hear sounds of children running past the house, then stillness.
Sudden memories flash in of my loved one's illness.
I then see the table and the object again.
Glitches of past and present, happiness and loss continue. Until I regain
My grounding. I try to not get held by the memories of a time gone by.
Their life was like flowers in Winter that fade no matter how hard you try.
There is coldness in this room now as they are not here.
A Summer chill has breathed heavily into the room I fear.
I shiver as I look up at the flickering bulb of light.
Wondering how, and if, I will sleep tonight.
I will always be their moon as they were the sun.
They reflected their goodness, warmth and power onto me in all they've done.
All that is left of them sits on this table.
I try to get up again, but I am truly unable.
I touch the object again; I see more memory flashes
Of love, of warmth, of illness, then they fade and all I see is my loved one's ashes.

Wesley Rolston – 1st Place

EPISODE 4

1st Place – Gerald Kells

EPISODE 5

1st Place – Lisa Millard

Big Sister

Imagine, a baby boy
as precious as porcelain
encased in a plastic box,
born two days, too late.

His fate, delicately balanced
on the fingertips of latex laced hands
a barely beating heart,
threatening to finish before it starts.

Imagine a mother,
whose searing pain is numb.
She cries into a stiff starched pillow
what will happen to her son?

Imagine a father,
whose actions are helpless.
Pacing for miles in fates waiting room,
basked in light,
as artificial as the nurse's sympathetic smiles.

Imagine a little girl,
oblivious to it all
unaware of the big sister
responsibility that will befall.

Her shoes squeak excitedly
as they tap down the hallway,
towards the little brother
who is unsure if he is going to stay.

Imagine, a white rabbit,
with a purple polka dot belly.
Passed from an innocent hand to hang
upon a life force machine.

A symbol that will stand the test of time
that, if he would fight to stay on Earth,
she would ensure that everything would be fine.

Lisa Millard – 1st Place

The Port 'N' Cigar Club Fund

Maiden aunts across the country, we beseech thee!
Don't give money to that nephew or that niece,
inside a card at Christmas or for birthdays:
the going rate being five pounds a piece.
Because the temptation to spend it, it's a grave one;
as intended, for a customary treat,
not on ladies of the night; on drugs or liquor,
but on outings to the zoo and bags of sweets.

But what you're doing; trust us, it is not a kindness,
'entrapment's' what we think you'll find it's called,
encouraging your kin to be so selfish
and t'think the government is that easily fooled.
They're not, and they will come down on them like a ton of bricks;
landed peers across the land will all be miffed,
if they don't proffer a pound in every fiver:
'unearned income' is the legal word for 'gift'.

But in a cash free society
not a penny slips through the net:
no cash in hand for the boys in the band
and your pocket money's under threat.
And the MP's favourite charity:
'The Port & Cigar Club Fund',
gets a welcome boost, as your accounts are juiced;
don't tell me you are shocked and stunned?

Going out for a soiree or a supper, indulging in hospitality,
enjoying something that we wouldn't have at home,
prepared to standards that are quite exemplary.
Receiving service that's above and beyond
what we have come to think of as the very least,
from a polite and friendly minimum wage worker,
whose hourly rate deserves to be increased.

It is a custom to recognise such efforts
with a gratuity of ten percent the bill:
a cash reward for services well rendered;
a transaction that does not go through the till.
But in doing so we find ourselves embroiled
in another plot to plunder and to strip,
the coffers of HMRC and The Treasury,
'cause 'unearned income' is the legal term for 'tip'.

But in a cash free society
not a penny slips through the net:
no cash in hand for the boys in the band,
and your pocket money's under threat.
And the MP's favourite charity:
'The Port & Cigar Club Fund',
gets a welcome boost, as your accounts are juiced;
and everyone is shocked and stunned.

If they take away our right to pay
with paper money and with coins,
and put it all online, so they can tax and fine,
freezing assets that they then purloin.
And the MP's favourite charity:
'The Port & Cigar Club Fund',
will control our lives from the day we arrive,
'til the day that they decide we're shunned.

Paul Eccentric – Special Guest

EPISODE SIX

1st Place – Claire Hughes

If Hope is the Thing with Feathers

after Emily Dickinson

As I sit, I wonder;
if Hope has feathers,
if it's a little bird
that sits perched
within the soul,
what form does it take?
What wings do shake?
What song does it make?

If it is even a bird,
surely it is absurd
to think it is
a Blackbird.
For though its song is sweet,
a treat in the early heat
of dawn –
its feathers are black
as death.
Smudges of coal
that toll the bells
of the Wild Hunt.

If it's decided that Hope's feathers
are not black,
then the odds are stacked against
the Jackdaw
the Rook
the Raven
and the Crow.

And what then of the Magpie?
With its streaks of teal and blue
like a great slew
of winter tide –
the tide, the tide, the sea,

can it be?
The wash of waves has always brought hope to me,
but no,
don't you see?
It has been decreed
that Mag Pie's feathers
belong
to Joy.

So do we toy with the idea
of dear old Robin Redbreast?
Whose red beat chest
looks best
in blooms
of winter snow.

It makes more sense
than the Crow
but somehow I know
it cannot be so
because they say
it appears
when loved ones are near.
So it too carries
the breath
of death
and no cloak
of hope.

I sit and toss each name
into the fire –
the Blue Tit
the Great Tit
the Sparrows
and the Pigeons,
the Doves
the Ducks
none of them help

with my decision.

I watch them curl and burn
with the Owl and the Wren
but then,
as they crumble to ash,
as they flitter to nothing,
I see a single bud of flame.
Then two,
then three,
they circle and grow
like a fresh spring tree.

It's then that I know,
as the wild flames blow,
that Hope is a burning bright
breath of light that blows
from pools of ash.
A dance of fire
that grips your bones
when you are thrown
into the pits
of despair.

It shares its warmth,
its song,
its strong
wealth of tears
to heal each fear
and clear
the debris,
of tragedy.

Now
I know,
as her wild flames blow,
that Hope
is a Phoenix.

Claire Hughes – 1st Place

EPISODE SEVEN

1st Place – Lisa Johnston

Choices

When two feet meet on street
Side by side
tarmac smiling wide
Hold back
Resist the blacktop slap
Choose small dirt track
That snaps back and claps
Step set to refresh and address
The lack of green
gone unseen
Too long missed out on the day's sweet song
So stride out
hear stones shout
With glass screech as they rub against another
small pebble brother
Teeth set on edge but smoothed by gleam of stream
Pause and dream with eyes half closed
Whilst rows of crows,
squawk talk, bob and nod
In black backed pairs
Coal eyes stare
Unaware of where
This path unwinds
It just climbs
to greet trees whilst
Leaves drop as patterned rug
And legs tugged at by breeze
lungs squeeze
out each and every drop
Before packed up again in box
Brought back across the blacktop
With barcode bleep
Delivered neat, streaked
With brown tape

draped, shaped to fit doorstep
Receipt kept
return marked across top
But no it'll stop
Be opened wide for inside brings the outside
Fresh air
Striped sky
bird call
memories filed
For rainy day slideshow recall

Lisa Johnston – 1st Place

EPISODE EIGHT

1st Place – Ashley Edge

Edge to Edge

We drove there in a horse box,
our possessions stacked
like Tetris pieces. Furniture
dismantled to kindling.
Books packed, preciously,
in boxes marked 'careful'.
Ornaments wrapped, carelessly,
in month old newspaper –
footy scores peeking
out of the box, light reading
as I camped, crammed precariously
between mum's wardrobe
and the Welsh dresser,
the vrooms of cars
on the motorway, my lullaby.

We drove there in a horse box,
a few yards still in him.
Ingrained scent of hay
and manure masked the smell
of our English terrace. A home
condensed to a space only
a horse
should fill.

We drove there in a horse box.
Manejamos hacia ti.
From the edge of England
to the edge of Spain,
we skim-read France in a panic.
Eyes overwhelmed by white-rock homes,
not a single red brick in sight.
Our bums bounced, fingers vibrating,
as we juddered, jittered,
quivered further South,
through the snow-less, perilous
Alpujarras, as the gear box
whined, rapidly died,
threatened to stop us

where we could see you
with binoculars, if only a cloud
would mask the blinding light,
the searing sun, for just
one moment.

We limped to you, in a horse box
Nosotros cojeamos hacia ti
First gear for the final fifty miles.
We hobbled, hot
from fear, from the blaring rays,
from him. Through the mirage
of adventure, we saw. We saw
death's pale, clawing hand
stretch down through sudden
clouds, cast a shadow over the coast.

Through winding, potholed dirt tracks,
our horse box groaned and whimpered.
As we turned up the steep, sandy
lane, faced the imposing gate,
I smelt you.
A morsel of a waft, masked
by the *pino negro*, salty sea wind,
his Dunhill cologne.

We sat there, the four musketeers,
in the cab of our horse box;
as it sighed, staggered, spluttered
over the threshold
to a chorus of cicadas.

We drove to you, in a horse box.
Manejamos hacia ti.
And I reached out my hand,
touched your frail, brown
arms. Your wrinkled, liver-spotted
cheek flushed, pressed
against mine, your heavy,
spasmodic breath on my neck.

We let the horse box rest,
as we filled the villa
with laughter and games.
It sat there, in the driveway,
gathering autumn dust,
pinecones scattered on its roof.

As the horse box slumbered,
your health improved.
Day one, I fed you yoghurt
at the dining room table.
Day seven, you fed you yoghurt,
my hand hovering, just in case.
Day twenty you asked for a pack of cards,
taught me Round-the-Clock and Patience.
Day thirty you had me reaching
to the topmost shelf, encouraged
me to read ridiculous passages
from your Mills and Boon collection.
Day forty we took you out,
showed you off to our amigos
in the village, made your wheelchair
do wheelies on the promenade
whilst you squealed with glee;
your eyes sparkling like you were ten again.
Day forty-one he intervened.

We left you, with the horse box.
Flew
Back
with empty hands, hollow hearts,
to the red-brick houses
sand-less lanes,
beach-less Midlands,
where we waited for the call,
the dreaded call.

Ashley Edge – 1st Place

Final Journey

Under a cloudless sky of tears
The journey began.
Her wee
The colour of rosé wine
Was the warning sign.
Waiting rooms, automatic doors
Fluorescent Lights, sombre discourse.

Not stage 1, 2 or 3
But stage 4.
The tumour cackled its
declaration of war.

And all she said was:
'I don't want to talk
I want to paddle in nippy seas.
Goose bumped but happy
And not fear this disease.
But embrace this blistered rot and scour
And don't you dare despair
Till my final hour.'

So she
Drove her veteran blue mini

Down thunder road.
Danced in the dark
Until she slowed.
Dreamt of spiralling mountain treks
Looking for herself beyond the apex.

Until the greedy cancer devoured her mass.
Though her soul was mighty
Her body was fragile like glass.
After a while she stated
'She was growing wings.'
Who knew if it was the morphine
Or the real thing?
Then
Over the cloudless sky of tears she soared.
To start the next chapter.
She had never liked being bored.

Angie Payne – 2nd Place

Fisherman's Moon

Leathery hand on sun roasted skin
His weathered head, it nods
A gentle salute to the amber moon
'Be generous beguiling loon'

Glassy eyes swim back and forth
Over the motionless silken sheet
Midnight blue bedding ripples
Beckoning the ready to sleep

Rickety platform to a warm wooden boat,
Creaks and neighs like a faithful horse
Singing- 'gentle laps, please, call him back'
'No one should be out so late'
the boat rocks with the fisherman's weight

Jaded hands guide jaded oars
Advance, rotate, release,
No land in sight. Soft sea - no fight

Long gone the hope of catching fish
Calm red face with rusty cracks
Reveals its folded secret, eternal wish

Holding a pebble in his weary palm,
It soothes his troubled hands
Smooth surface emits its calm
Abandoned fingers cling on tight
Mutineers, untrustworthy friends

Mustering a long-forgotten force, he throws
Gone with a gulp, that stone, so deep
Oars now out of reach

His head rests on a torn net
His insignificant life halloed
His eyes close.

A gull silhouetted by the golden sky orb
Heralds his journey down a moonlit path.

Joanna Smart – Commended Open Mic Poet

That day

(in memory of the 19 girls and young women
who died in Dudley Port 6th March 1922)

Previously published in Multistory as part of Tipton Tales

6.00am give or take
Maybe she got up, still frowsy with sleep,
babby sister stirring as she creeps out
of the bed they share. Bare feet padding down
the stairs. Huffing out freezing plumes of air,
appearing in the kitchen where mom pokes at
lazy coal. The coal her step-brothers picked
yesterday off the bonk. And maybe dad
is sitting in shame or a wing-backed chair
up early as if there was still a job
to go to. And maybe he did say 'Oh, bab...
doh goo today. S'no job for a wench.'
Perhaps Edith smiled, said she could earn
enough to pay the rent. I'd like to think
he put a hand to the child's head as she
bent to lace her hobnail boots. And I'd like
to think she looked up and smiled at him
before she headed off up Factory Road
into the cold smog of a March morning.

Between 7 and 8
I think she whistled as she walked. Waved
to Mr Davies standing on the front step
of the Fountain. I like to think that Mr Davies
(a Woodbine hanging from his lip) waved back.
Maybe our Edith called for Edith Drew
or Nellie Kay, giggling all the way
from Tipton up to Dudley Port.
Cheeking lads who crossed their paths.
Yes, I'd like to think they laughed.

8 am on the dot
The workshop was freezing I should imagine
even with a small stove burning. I expect

they blew on their hands from time to time
as they pushed cartridges through holes
in metal boxes, where with a deft twist
of their agile fingers the young wenches
wrenched free the paper-thin copper
(which might have been the self same colour
as Lizzie Griffiths' hair). I'll bet they bantered
as they separated metals from live ammo
and gunpowder peppered the floor, their clothes.
And I'll bet they rolled their eyes when
Gladys Bryant's mom came to complain
about low wages! *Who's 'er think her is, eh?*
Putting a flea in the ear of management.
Maybe they sang or song or two. Passing hours.

11.45 or thereabouts
I'll bet bellies had been grumbling for a while
not so far off dinnertime. Perhaps Edith heard
the fizz that one girl had reported. I hope she did
and then I hope she heard no more. Not the bang
that blew the roof to kingdom come and sent
the windows flying out. Or that unholy shrieking
as girls ran out to burn in an open yard

Emma Purshouse – Special Guest
Wolverhampton Poet Laureate 2019 – 2021

EPISODE NINE

1st Place – Phillip Knight

A Terraced House, Bolebridge Tamworth 1884

Martha lifted the guttering candle
as if in lifting it, she lifted herself
from the sepia sewage water
circling her heels, like a rabid dog
in high state of fever.

Biting cold as sharp as a rat's bite,
guttersnipes with black eyes,
she feared rats above anything else;
feared rats even more than the filth
at her laced booted feet.

Martha pinched her nose with
her free hand, mouth shut tight
trying to curb the stench from
flooding her aged lungs,
the Tame on her tongue.

Shouts, cries from the street,
a bell ringing 'unclean, unclean'.
'Evacuate! Evacuate! All tenants to leave.
Evacuate! All tenants to leave.
Bring no possessions!'

Martha tied in her woollen shawl,
as if tying it in would keep her safe,
extinguished the candle, hitched
up her linen skirt and tip-toed
through the rising menace.

Jan Hedger – 3rd Place

Happy Child

Your smile shines out on this dull
day and your cheeks glow after playing
with friends. The wind has been
bitingly cold and the sun has been hiding,

but you didn't notice; you were too busy
giggling when your friend Izzy pretending
to be a pig with a stocking-tail. She ran,
grunted and chased you all until it began
to hail; hammering down on your heads.

You all screamed and hid in the shed,
then ran out with plant pots on your
heads
when it stopped. You became brown bears
growling and stamping until now,
because even bears need their tea.

Janet Jenkins – Special Guest: The Lichfield Poets

On the Beach

Yellow fog of stale breath
from cavities of corruption;
stink of something rotten,
cold dead hands of kelp
grasping broken rubbish;
gannet's thin skull
splinters under foot.

Waves thrash strand
to jagged shingle;
broken glass, bleached plastic,
nails from wrecked boats;
this sea knows its business
which is to drown
all the dry world.

Strip yourself, leave your skin
for other scavengers;
as nothing you can slip
through water's tight knit bond
into such minuteness
of infinity that you'll become
something entirely new.

Sarah Dale – Special Guest: The Lichfield Poets

Embryo

Love nurtured you,
Each day bringing change,
A secret unseen fusion.

Pink limbs budding,
An embryonic ammonite,
Protected in amniotic sac.

Secluded, concealed,
A strange merger and cleaving,
Zygote, structure, form.

A primitive thing,
Nodal, yolked, implanted-
The first shunting of blood

Through atrium, ventricle, heart.
Blossom unfurling, fluttering of lungs,
Dermis, brain-cells, nerves.

This fledgling, roundel, swelling,
Deeply held within maternal space,
Safer than you will ever be again.

A twisted baptism through water, blood,
Until the final flowering of you-
Rich with golden pollen-dust.

Susan Wood – Special Guest: The Lichfield Poets

EPISODE TEN – SEASON THREE GRAND FINAL

1st Place – Hannah Brockley

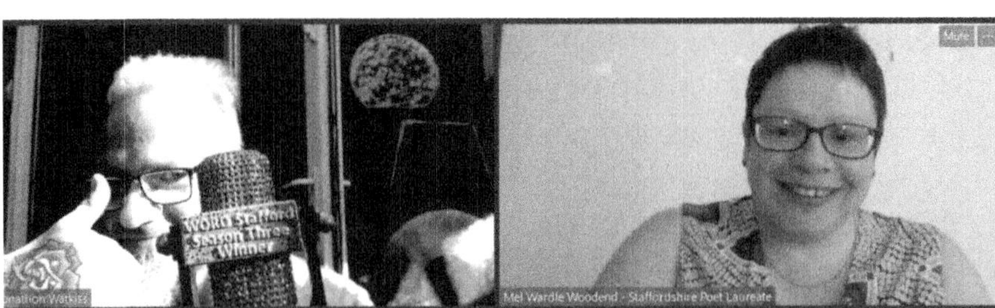

Blind Johnny Smoke and Mel Wardle Woodend
at
Season Three Episode Ten Grand Final on Zoom

How Can We Trust the System

When someone mentions the police,
what thoughts come to your mind?
Which, of all the injustices
they have committed,
do you think of first?
How can we trust
the system which allegedly
protects us, when innumerable cases
show its incompetence,
its violence, its complete and absurd
sense of superiority and power?

In 2021, Sarah Everard
was not only kidnapped,
but murdered by Wayne Couzens,
a Met Police officer.
When she was mourned,
remembered, respected and loved,
police officers abused, hurt
and violently ended
the vigil which lamented
and condemned the horrors
Sarah was subjected to.

Why was Benjamin Kemp
not prosecuted, when he
struck a disabled teenage girl
more than 30 times after
spraying her face with CS spray?

Why was George Floyd
discriminated, violently
attacked, suffocated and murdered
by Derek Chauvin, while he begged
for mercy, yelling:

"Mom, love you. Tell my kids
I love them. I'm dead.?"

Remember these
murderers' names.
Remember police brutality,
remember their violence,
their complete ineptitude,
their lack of humanity and empathy.
Remember it all,
for the only way to move forward
is by never forgetting their crimes.

Daniel Kay – Commended Open Mic Poet

Ciudad de Sevilla

"El Real Alcazar de Sevilla es uno de palacios
En mas antigues de mundo"

Sharp, citrus lemons mingle
With the scent of old plaster.
Pervading fragrance of orange blossom
Orange trees, musky and intense.

Plaza Nueva, cobbled square
Lined with tall buildings
Gilded in sunshine.
Al fresco bars inviting
Taste buds, juices flow for
Savoury, spicy, tapas.
Terracotta sangria jugs
Gleaming rows of glasses
Absorb the colours, flavours
Of Seville's sensuality.

Waves of sound as fingers
Strummed, plucked and rippled
Guitarist hand lashing out
To the instrument's body
Across taught strings.

Dancers' feet moving in rhythm
Red shoes tapped and clipped
Dress clinging, trailing on the ground
Eyes Smokey, dark curls hanging down
Her back, shiny and free.

Intimate, seductive, heat
Suffusing her body
Transported to another world
Rising to a crescendo
Taking the audience with her
In a frenetic climax.

Pauline Faulkner – Commended Open Mic Poet

Defences

Life size 17-year-old comes complete with all the deluxe defence mechanisms: denial, satire and self-sabotage.

Examples of programmed movements include dealing with mental health issues by not participating in education,
Toy will do anything to avoid admitting to internal faults and malfunctions including breaking directives,
Because who wants a computational probe?
So I'll be seconds away from tapping the send button on my college withdrawal with tears streaming down my face,
Feeling like I've got no future or future of feeling,

See also making jokes about being a professional dancer when presented with a diagnosis of physical decline,
Items may say unbreakable but that only counts for the parts you can see,
And is smile may be wide but it's painted, unchanging no matter the situation,
So yes things maybe dire and I am as uncomfortable as everyone else,
But I'd rather make you laugh awkwardly than let the reality sink in.

Last but not least auditioning for long programs away from home despite inaccessibilities,
Figure is unable to cross uneven ground, climb steep inclines or use steps and stairs,
Despite that why shouldn't I move to London alone with no support network for a year,
Carers. I'll cross that bridge when I come to it and I'm sure the tube assistance is always top notch just like the parking in York,
What's that mum, reality? I don't want that

Fixed poses include hands over the ears, hands over the eyes and curling up in a ball,
Phrases include it'll be fine, I don't care, nothing and 'the grunt',
The confidence advertised on the box might malfunction if you read the small print,
Holes may appear if interacted with beyond the plastic screen,
And may be expected to turn on manufacturers in response to environmental struggles.

Kizzy Wade – Wild Card (Poet the most times placed 2nd or 3rd all Season)

JUDGES'

POEMS

Seashell

Seawater drips from my fingertips,
sand grains cling to my damp toes,
glittering dancing slippers.
Taking a single fragile pearly shell from the water's edge,
its gentle serrations imprinting the sand,
I clamber rough steps
from this perfect beach
to you, for you.

King-like you gaze from your parapet
surveying our wondrous realm,
smelling the sea, hearing the heaving waves,
inaccessible expanse of paradise,
my outstretched palm gifting you the ocean
in a tiny seashell.

Sandra Mary Chambers

Loss

I felt lost today.
There was a sad romanticism hanging in
the air,
And my palms curled in,
Out,
Sweaty and wet
with tears.
Inside my heart a joy was
kindled with the
spirits floating in my brain

and I think
they'll never stop whistling.
Their song is a melancholy
heartland, a fallen angel in
a fire of bliss.
And if they stop,
I'll feel the loss again,
but stronger and deeper
and darker than the silence has
ever been before.

Lily Massey

Staffordshire Young Poet Laureate 2018 – 2019

Flowers

When you were in full bloom
You brought such splendour to this room
Vibrant red and juicy green
Most beautiful I'd ever seen

Falling petals day by day
Before it showed I sensed decay
Couldn't live with the suspense
No more water, vain attempts

Soon your colours fade to grey
Peace at last, now you may stay

Uschi Wheeler

Ocean Whispers

I stand on the sand, the ocean lolling around my feet,
I look up admiring what is in front of me.
I close my eyes, block all sound out except for the
Gentle lapping going on around me.

I open my eyes and breathe deeply, the smell
That I love so much. I am home.
Gazing at the vast ocean before me,
I can hear it calling.

So blue, unlike anything that I have ever seen,
Clear, you can see all the way through.
My friend and I go on a boat trip, precious memories,
Seals, dolphins and more, even a man o war!

Mesmerized by it all, I want to explore.

Later again, standing by the shore,
It calls me once more.
Step by step, I go in, the water swallowing me whole.
I am home.

Stress and tension dissipate, all cares gone,

The ocean and I swim as one, I come up for air,

So relaxed and unwinding, I feel free.

The ocean, so blue it is comforting,

Splashing and swimming around, the waves start to build up,

crashing around,

The lifeguards shout and we come out, happy and content as can be.

Until tomorrow my dear ocean,

Another day arises, beautiful, in awe, I step out of the door,

Seagulls squawking away, ducking and diving as they devour their

Precious feast. A gift from the ocean.

I sit, cup of coffee in hand, Admiring the scenery before me,

The air tastes extra salty, I lick my lips in delight,

Whilst my friend laughs and pretends to roll her eyes.

"What are you like?" she says. She knows me too well.

The weather changes slightly, a storm is coming,

Today we cannot bask in the almighty ocean's glow.

The waves come in thick and fast, building up and up to great heights.

It is all-consuming, destruction of everything that gets in its path,

I stand watching the waves crash, not believing that not more than two minutes ago,

Everything was still. I am in awe. An hour later, the white horses still roar,

It is deafening but beautiful still. Hypnotic and chaotic, the ocean releases its beast.

Afternoon comes, all is still, the ocean is safe once more,

I feel the pull and I have to go in, needing freedom once again.

The day we leave, I wave a sad goodbye, as the wind rushes through my hair,

The ocean whispers to me "I will see you again." I nod in agreement, hoping that

with all my might it may be soon.

My heart weeps as I know that I belong in the sea, even when I am not there, the pull is strong.

The ocean is where I belong.

Katy Watkiss

SOMETHING

FROM THE

HOSTS

Grenfell 2017 – 2019

In June 2017 an obscene scene
flashed across our TV screens
leaving the world in shock
as firefighters worked around the clock

at great risk to their own lives again and again, the men and
women of the London fire brigade rushed into the flames
trying to reach people to save.
They were just doing their jobs but these heroes behaved in a way
that was incredibly, exceptionally brave.
Now after the event the flames have died down yet the country is
enraged, inflamed
because these exceptionally brave men and women are being
blamed

and I think it's exceptionally disgusting - you see
the fire service is accused of having incorrect advice on their
information sheets:
fire procedures that say stay put, stay where you are in the event
of a fire
because the flats are self-contained and the flames can't spread
higher

and that's what everybody thought because at the time the
innocent people who lost their lives
and the fire service did not realise
that the snooty big wigs in the nearby more affluent
neighbourhood didn't like the look of Grenfell's grey exteriors
where it stood.
They only wanted to see pretty colours in the world and to turn a
blind eye to their neighbours in poverty if they could

so they dressed the building in a shiny new suit and it stood
proudly clad for a while
until the night of the Grenfell fire.
Residents awoke in a furnace instead of a block of flats.
The people of Grenfell Tower didn't stand a chance

Yet politicians have hastened to say
that if they had been in the fire they wouldn't have been affected in
that way!

They assumed that tower blocks are full of people with lower
intelligence than all the Tories who debate.
Oh wait! It's not assumed it's exactly what they state:

'If you or I were in a fire we would have the common sense to
leave a burning building' (a Tory politician said to an interviewer
on live TV).
This contemptuous class-based statement sickens me.
I doubt these condescending creatures have ever set foot in a
tower block,
they are probably too scared to meet 'real people'; it would be a
shock

to learn the world does not only contain over-indulged individuals
like their Tory friends
but real people who are sometimes a bit rough around the edge,
who might not have had the best opportunities, who might not
have much money to meet their ends:
real people with real lives,
real babies, real pets, real partners and real relatives who
watched on TV hoping and praying they would survive.
Real hearts that beat and stopped.

What would you do if in the early hours of the morning you woke
from sleep in fright
with the petrifying realisation your block was alight?
Would you 1: Race out of your flat to the stairs - where there are
white hot flames, choking smoke and burning air?
Or 2: Stay in your flat (as instructed by all the fire procedures
labelled on notices around your building) - because your flat, your
HOME, your cocoon is supposed to be a fireproof unit?
I know what I'd do,
number 2

because in other high rise blocks it's the same,
the fire notices everywhere explain
and they've all been checked
rigorously since Grenfell – it's what you'd expect.

They say that unless the fire is in your flat you should stay put
because all the walls and floors
between flats are concrete and the flats all have fireproof doors
so essentially each flat should be a concrete fireproof bunker

where you can wait for rescue, batten down the hatches, hunker.

At Grenfell people could not escape; there was no chance
as the cladding enhanced hellish flames that licked their way up
the building and Satanically danced.
Other blocks have had previous fires but I'm glad to say
the concrete structures kept everyone safe because of the way
they are made,

the fire brigade could put out the fire in the flat where it was
detected
and the other residents in the block remained - unaffected.
I'd imagine Grenfell were built the same just like many of the
period. The difference is other blocks remain on skylines just as
they were made –
a little bit ugly, dull, drab, and grey

but they are functional, homes, and hopefully safe
with no need to be dressed up in colourful cladding just to
appease a neighbourhood who think it's an eyesore - an aesthetic
disgrace.
The difference is not that people in tower blocks have less
common sense than other members of society;
that's a ridiculously, snobby, class centred statement from
politicians showing their perceived class hierarchy.

No. The difference is that the rich big wigs in their posh area of
London disliked
a plain and honest concrete structure on their skyline - because it
offended their eyes.
They couldn't stand the grey reality of a building the less wealthy
live in so wrapped it in colourful cladding for their own ends.
The company who made the cladding, the people who deemed
the cladding safe, those who wanted the cladding fit and the
politicians are the ones with no common sense.

Where is the empathy?
Where is the sadness in their eyes
for those who lost someone they love
and the victims who have died?

Mel Wardle Woodend (2019)

Tin

From under a frown, I utter…
'Put that tin down. Back away from the shelf, leave that last one for somebody else. Your basket already doth overflow, hang your greedy head in shame and on you go'.

How dirty is your anus that you need 48 bog rolls in the next few days, mend your ways,
your diet must be wrong and your kecks must pong. Put those beans back, you don't need any more fibre if that's what's inside ya.

Of which castle are you the king, that you need so many things, more so than me mum and dad, or that little old lady you've made look so sad, as you beat her to the last loaf of bread, don't be a knob, let her have it instead.

As you load up your shiny car, take a moment to think how far, some of us are away from essential supplies, and that while you're hoarding, someone else vulnerable might die.

All the hand sanitiser in the world won't cleanse your grubby mind, of your greedy ways, of your acts unkind, everyone for themselves as you decimate the shelves so there's bugger all left for me and my essential delivery.

You see, I'm stuck inside, on the advice of the wise, so for food shopping I'm a bit stuck, but it's not like you give a… rat's clinker, you're behaving like a winker. Shame on you.

Being blind I'd normally catch the bus, I don't mind, don't make a fuss. Two bags in my right hand is my limit you see, guide dog in my left hand, because, you see? I can't, very well. But it's not a sob story I tell.

Because I'm lucky. I've got mates, I've got friends, and I know that the world isn't going to end. We look after each other, because we can, and we want to, not like you, not like you, and this selfish hoarding that you do.

My friends keep dropping by, with bits and bobs for our modest supplies, and we smile thankfully and wave, from inside our isolated cave, while we batten down our hatches, missing gigs and football matches, but we're safe, we'll get by.

But we'd get by with a little bit more food in our house, if you hadn't been such a bulk buying lout. Your pantry may bulging with beans, and your freezer might be groaning cos you're mean. But there's one thing that occurs to me, that your soul must be quite empty. Quite lacking in empathy as you parade the darker side of humanity, down that aisle.

So put that bloody tin down, you clown. Put that extra butt wipe back, you twat. Go home and lock yourself away, and don't come back for a couple of days, mend your ways, you utter swine.
I hope the rest of us will be kind, think of others, and not be selfish buggers. When we come out of the other side of this, for those around me, I'll have a shake of hands, a hug, a kiss.

But for your I'll have a scowl, a frown, because you wouldn't put that last tin down. Idiot.

Blind Johnny Smoke (2020)

OTHER

THINGS

Throughout the Seasons (and actual seasons) we created and took part in lots of other events in addition to our regular WORD Episodes.

These have included:

STAFFORD WALKING STREET

With Guide Dog / Poetry Dog JJ

POSITIVE POETRY AND POEMS

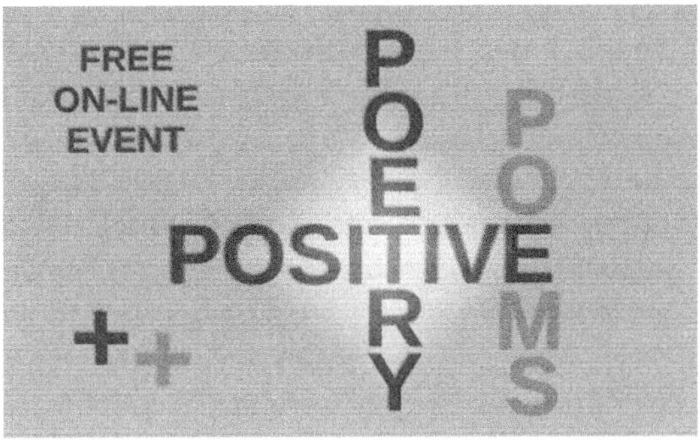

WORLD BOOK NIGHT

STAFFORDSHIRE DAY

MYTHS AND LEGENDS

MENTAL HEALTH AWARENESS WEEK

WORD
STAFFORD A 'ZOOM' EVENT

BE
KIND

The Mental Health Foundation's Mental Health Awareness Week will take place from 18-24 May 2020 promoting the theme of kindness.

Join WORD Stafford for a 'kindness' themed mental health awareness poetry night with a talk on Bibliotherapy and Poetry Therapy by the Staffordshire Poet Laureate - followed by an open mic session.

MONDAY
18TH JUNE
7 - 9PM

Please contact melwoodendwriting@gmail.com to take part.

https://www.mentalhealth.org.uk/campaigns/mental-health-awareness-week

WORLD OCEANS DAY

EMPATHY DAY

#EMPATHY DAY
9 June 2020
empathylab.uk

WO
RD Stafford & Staffordshire Libraries
present:

'Empathy Day' 9 June 2020

An on line spoken word event 7-9 pm

Hear a brand new 'empathy' poem by the Staffordshire Poet Laureate and explore Empathy Day with WORD Stafford in association with Staffordshire Libraries, through a Zoom online open mic night of thoughtfully constructed, empathy focused poetry from 7pm-9pm

'Empathy Day helps us understand each other better by using books to step into someone else's shoes. When you read, your brain reacts as it would to real events. This makes books the perfect empathy boosting vehicle...'

YOUR LIBRARY
Staffordshire County Council

WORLD POETRY DAY BOOK LAUNCH

We even published a book of World Poetry Day poems from WORD Stafford poets and the Stone Scribblers

THE FESTIVAL OF HOPE

When Lockdown lifted we were invited to take part in The Festival of Hope at Penkridge Middle School,

BLACK LIVES MATTER

held an evening of poetry and spoken word in solidarity with Black Lives Matter, with headline poetry performances and a talk by Jason N Smith and iLikeZach,

ALZHEIMER'S AWARENESS POETRY NIGHT

DYSLEXIA AWARENESS POETRY NIGHT

an evening of poetry shared to raise awareness of Alzheimer's Disease, and a Dyslexia Awareness Spoken Word Event with a talk and poetry by special guest Helen Kay.

NATIONAL POETRY DAY

For National Poetry Day 2020, the theme was 'Vision' so we decided to curate and publish a photopoetry anthology of ekphrastic poetry in support of Guide Dogs.

We held a book launch on Zoom on National Poetry Day and were supported by Staffordshire Libraries, WORD poets who had contributed to the book and a wonderful online audience.

COMPETITIONS

We held poetry writing competitions with book prizes purchased from our special guests,

CHRISTMAS PARTY

and even held a Christmas Party on Zoom.

Looking back, we made the best of things - all joking about bringing our own booze and mince pies to the screen - but really given the choice I think we all missed pre-pandemic face to face events.

Zoom did keep us sane though, as it allowed us to stay connected through the darkest days of each Lockdown until we could tentatively start moving back into face to face – and even new hybrid events – as we moved into Season Four.

BONUS MATERIAL – ECHOES POETRY FILM

Our poetry film 'Echoes' can be viewed by typing the following link into your internet address bar

https://l.facebook.com/l.php?u=https%3A%2F%2Fyoutu.be%2FRZWw3sq8peY%3Ffbclid%3DIwAR3Oz-6OcLxzdPHvODNDyqJA-S5GkC0zCyl4RMOuJvPvUOCcD0rgwuzYG1Y&h=AT1n5GhVeOjnTpq_MjrETuf04CiRVGYyMR_pKF_1_xnEqsg0es2Ai2d6s_89nxd1FBfw_F-MnMwtOWtmvt_0ZbKwBv5xTslnG1RnNRVHN8McVinoOLQKVMUTjPe7qWQPqpl

Or by scanning the QR code.

'Echoes' was created as part of The Pocket Film Festival 2020 with words written and performed by Mel Wardle Woodend and music, sound, visuals and editing by Blind Johnny Smoke.

BIOGRAPHIES

Mel Wardle Woodend is Staffordshire Poet Laureate 2019-2022 and Director of dyslexia friendly publishing company Dream Well Writing Ltd: reflecting her passion for making reading and books accessible and enjoyable to as many people as possible.

Her own published poetry collections include *Natural Colours* (2017), *Just a Thought* (2019), several children's books, a short story published in paperback *Tabitha* (2021), poetry anthology *One Hundred Memories* (2019) in support of Alzheimer's Society, and *Poetic Vision* (2020) for Guide Dogs UK.

Mel holds an MA in Creative Writing and enjoys facilitating poetry workshops, slams and open-mic events. She is co-organiser of WORD Stafford: a popular regular spoken word night currently in its fourth season. Mel is Creative Director of Stafford Literature Festival 2022.

Jon Watkiss AKA Blind Johnny Smoke is a founder member of UK electro punk act Flesh Eating Foundation, half of spoken word power electronics duo The Mannequin Factory, gong soundscapers Men With Mallets and weird electronica act Sideblinder. He also creates regular improvised soundscapes and chips in with the Murmurists collective when he can. Additionally, he is a deaf/blind filmmaker/photographer and soundtracker.

He runs regular poetry events as 'WORD Stafford' with Mel Wardle Woodend and is a keen supporter of all grass roots art forms.

ABOUT WORD STAFFORD

WORD is a regular event combining a poetry slam, open mic and spoken word performance. Usually held at venues in the county town of Stafford, WORD Stafford is Stafford's only regular spoken word event, and additionally involves online events, videos, and competitions to enter.

WORD Stafford is organised by Mel Wardle Woodend and Blind Johnny Smoke.

Find out more about WORD Stafford at

https://www.facebook.com/WORDstafford/

DREAM WELL WRITING LTD

Dream Well Writing Ltd are Staffordshire based publishers of dyslexia friendly books – with worldwide distribution and an environmentally conscious ethos – founded in 2017 by Mel Wardle Woodend Staffordshire Poet Laureate 2019 – 2022.

Find out more about Dream Well at

http://dreamwellwriting.simplesite.com/

https://www.facebook.com/dreamwellwriting/

dreamwellwriting@gmail.com

Printed in Great Britain
by Amazon

86866968R00079